Where Babies Play

written by Hayley Novak
illustrated by Joey Hannaford

HARCOURT BRACE & COMPANY

Orlando Atlanta Austin Boston San Francisco Chicago Dallas New York
Toronto London

Where does this little one play?

Where does this little one play?

Where does this little one play?

Where does this little one play?
On mother's lap!